BROTHERS AT WAR
– A FIRST WORLD WAR FAMILY HISTORY

By Sarah Ridley
With help from Eliza

FRANKLIN WATTS
LONDON • SYDNEY

First published in 2012 by Franklin Watts
Text copyright © Sarah Ridley 2012

Franklin Watts
338 Euston Road
London NW1 3BH

Franklin Watts Australia
Level 17/207 Kent Street
Sydney, NSW 2000

Editor: Sarah Peutrill
Designer: Jane Hawkins
Photographer: Jonathan Doyle, unless otherwise credited
Consultant: James Taylor

With thanks to Imperial War Museums and Lavenham Church.

This book would not have been possible without the generosity of Lionel Baker,
Jane Orbell and John Baker, for which many thanks. Also thanks to Earls Colne
Grammar School Old Boys Association and Lavenham Guildhall Museum.

Dewey number 940.4'00922'41

ISBN 978 1 4451 0870 4

Printed in China

Franklin Watts is a division of Hachette Children's Books,
an Hachette UK company.
www.hachette.co.uk

Picture credits
Lionel Baker: front cover tc, tr, bl, br, back cover cl, inside 1tc, 1tr, 3br, 4c, 4-5b,
5tcl, 5tc, 5tr, 6tl, 6cl, 6cr, 6bl, 6bc, 6br, 7cr, 7br, 10t, 11b, 12tl, 12tlb, 12tc, 13t,
16t, 17b, 20b, 21t, 22c, 23t, 23b, 24t, 25br, 27bl, 30t, 30cl, 30cr. Lionel Baker/
Jonathan Doyle: front cover tl, blb, bca, bc, bcb, bcr, back cover ca, ccl, c, cr, inside
1tl, 2t, 2ct, 2b, 3bl, 3bc, 5tl, 7bc, 9t, 10c, 21b, 22t, 22b, 25t, 25bl, 26b, 27br.
Jonathan Doyle: 4t, 28t, 28b. Copyright © Imperial War Museums: front cover
background Q3014, back cover background Q3014, 1 background Q3014, 8c
Q60695, 8-9b Q42033, 9cr PST2734, 10br PST6543, 12c Q33707, 12b Q33700,
13c Q30064, 13b Q33295, 14t Q54352, 14c CO2533, 14bl Q4846,
14br HU65494, 15b Q635, 16bl Q50687, 16br Q50445, 17t Q4115,
18t Q23, 18b CO802, 19t Q739, 19b Q1142, 20t Q5732,
23cl E(AUS)921, 23cr Q6431, 24cl Q2024, 24cr Q2049,
24bl Q5118, 24br Q3871, 26t Q55479, 29t Q31488.
Lavenham Guildhall Museum: 9cl. Sally Morgan/Ecoscene: 29b.
Museum of English Rural Life/University of Reading: 10bl, 11t.
PRO/Crown Copyright: 7t. By Kind Permission of
Suffolk Records Office: 21c.

*Every attempt has been made to clear copyright. Should there be any
inadvertent omission please apply to the publisher for rectification.*

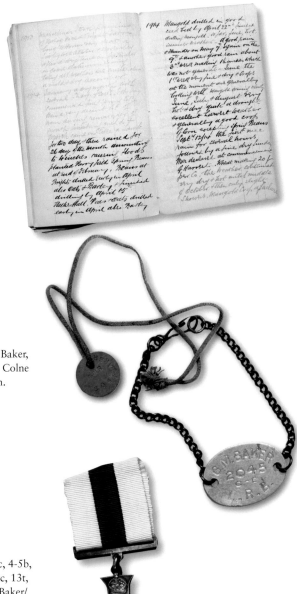

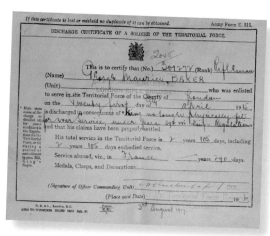

CONTENTS

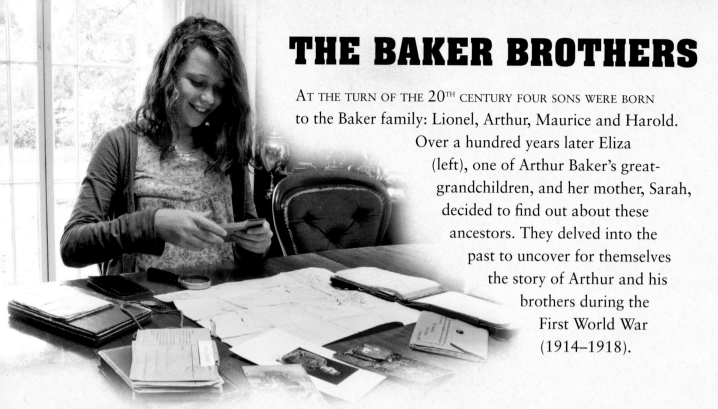

THE BAKER BROTHERS

At the turn of the 20th century four sons were born to the Baker family: Lionel, Arthur, Maurice and Harold. Over a hundred years later Eliza (left), one of Arthur Baker's great-grandchildren, and her mother, Sarah, decided to find out about these ancestors. They delved into the past to uncover for themselves the story of Arthur and his brothers during the First World War (1914–1918).

COUNTRY BOYS

The story starts in Lavenham, Suffolk, during the 1890s. John Baker's wife, Ada, gave birth to Lionel in 1893, Arthur in 1895, Maurice in 1897 and Harold in 1901. When the Baker brothers were growing up they enjoyed a secure childhood. Their father was a miller and farmer, while their mother looked after them and the house. They went to school, caught childhood illnesses and recovered from them, played sport and went to the seaside in the summer.

▶ Arthur, Maurice and Lionel Baker are the three little boys in the front row of this photo. It shows a big family gathering of aunts, uncles and cousins.

◀ The boys' father owned these windmills on the edge of Lavenham in partnership with his brother. The photo was taken in the 1880s.

MEMORIES AND ARTEFACTS

By talking to members of their family about the Baker brothers, some details of their lives have become clear to Eliza and her mother. In addition, letters, diaries, army forms and other family material have survived from the First World War and Eliza's Great-Uncle Lionel keeps them safe. He has generously shared this material to help build up the story in this book.

ELIZA'S FAMILY TREE

This is a simple version of Eliza's family tree, showing Eliza and her brothers at the bottom and tracing back her connection to the Baker brothers born a hundred years earlier. Details of her first cousins, second cousins and many aunts and uncles have been omitted for space.

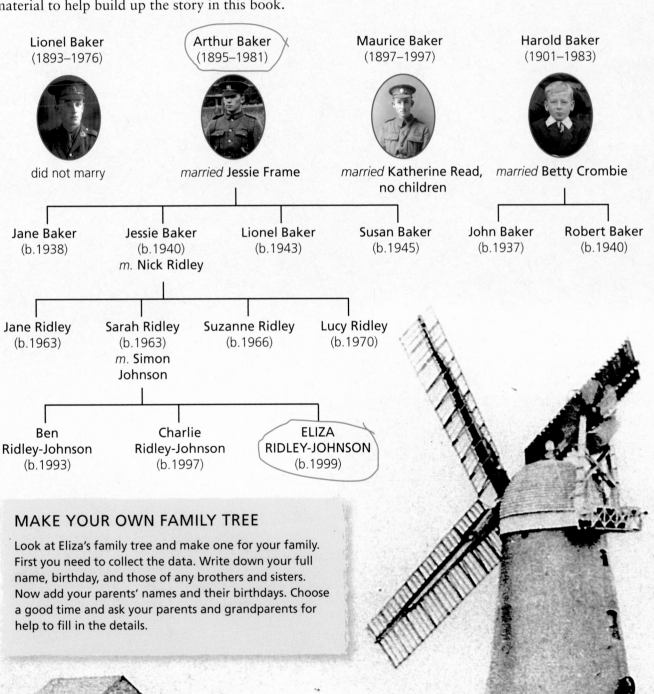

Lionel Baker
(1893–1976)

did not marry

Arthur Baker
(1895–1981)

married **Jessie Frame**

Maurice Baker
(1897–1997)

married **Katherine Read,
no children**

Harold Baker
(1901–1983)

married **Betty Crombie**

Jane Baker
(b.1938)

Jessie Baker
(b.1940)
m. **Nick Ridley**

Lionel Baker
(b.1943)

Susan Baker
(b.1945)

John Baker
(b.1937)

Robert Baker
(b.1940)

Jane Ridley
(b.1963)

Sarah Ridley
(b.1963)
m. **Simon
Johnson**

Suzanne Ridley
(b.1966)

Lucy Ridley
(b.1970)

**Ben
Ridley-Johnson**
(b.1993)

**Charlie
Ridley-Johnson**
(b.1997)

**ELIZA
RIDLEY-JOHNSON**
(b.1999)

MAKE YOUR OWN FAMILY TREE

Look at Eliza's family tree and make one for your family. First you need to collect the data. Write down your full name, birthday, and those of any brothers and sisters. Now add your parents' names and their birthdays. Choose a good time and ask your parents and grandparents for help to fill in the details.

A COUNTRY CHILDHOOD

At her great-uncle's home in Lavenham, Eliza looked at photos of her Great-Grandfather and his brothers as children. There are not many of them but they give a glimpse of their lives.

◀ Arthur, Maurice and Lionel (left to right) attended a fancy dress party in 1903.

▲ All four brothers appear in this photo taken around 1907 (Lionel, Maurice, Arthur back row, Harold in front).

▲ Lionel, his cousin, mother and aunt were photographed in a pony and trap parked in the mill's yard around 1897.

'HOME'

Eliza visited the house where the brothers grew up, Mill House, 45 Prentice Street, Lavenham. Behind the house is the flour mill, rebuilt by the brothers' father and uncle in 1893 and now converted to flats and houses. The boys would have heard this steam-powered mill in operation and also seen the Baker windmills in action on the outskirts of Lavenham. From home they could reach the countryside and the fields owned by their father, walk to church and visit friends and family who lived in Lavenham. From the train station at the other end of Lavenham, they travelled to school and sometimes to London, to visit family.

▼ The Baker family no longer own the mill, shown here in a drawing made in 1893 (below, left), or Mill House, Prentice Street (below, middle).

▶ Eliza visits Mill House as part of her research.

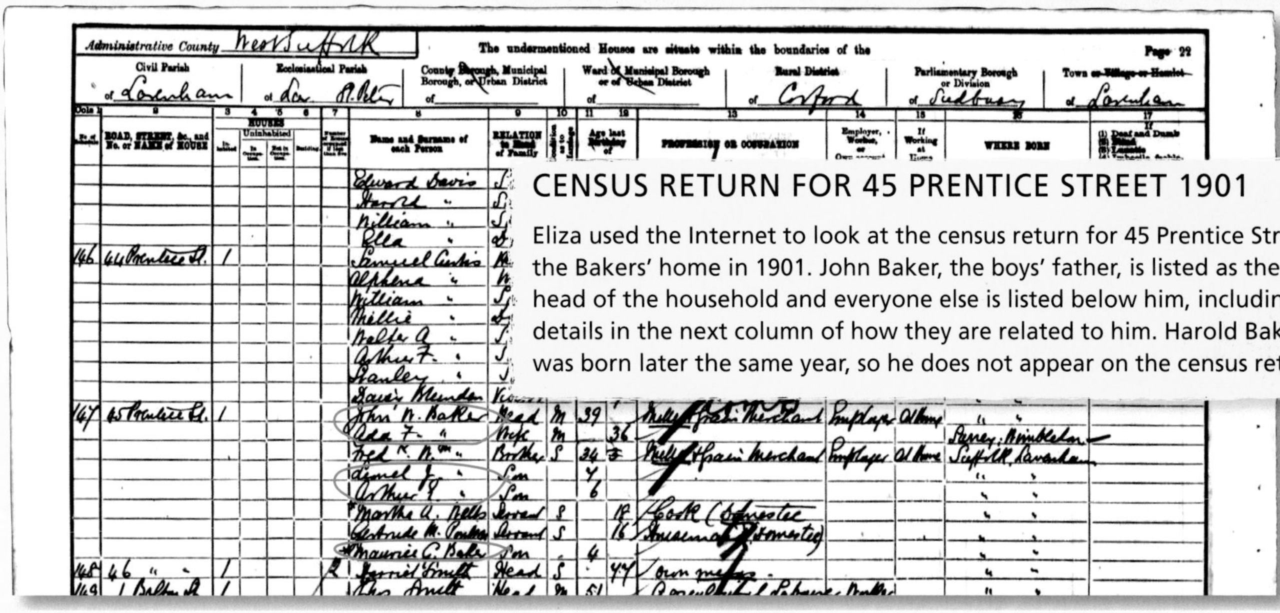
Administrative County West Suffolk
The undermentioned Houses are situate within the boundaries of the
Page 22
Civil Parish of Lavenham
Ecclesiastical Parish
County Borough, Municipal Borough, or Urban District
Ward of Municipal Borough or of Urban District
Rural District of Cosford
Parliamentary Borough or Division of Sudbury
Town or Village or Hamlet of Lavenham
ROAD, STREET, &c., and No. or NAME of HOUSE
HOUSES
Name and Surname of each Person
RELATION to Head of Family
PROFESSION OR OCCUPATION
WHERE BORN

CENSUS RETURN FOR 45 PRENTICE STREET 1901

Eliza used the Internet to look at the census return for 45 Prentice Street, the Bakers' home in 1901. John Baker, the boys' father, is listed as the head of the household and everyone else is listed below him, including details in the next column of how they are related to him. Harold Baker was born later the same year, so he does not appear on the census return.

SCHOOL DAYS

The Baker brothers went to infant school, then to the grammar school in Earls Colne in Essex. They had to board (live at school) as it was too far to travel there daily. Eliza's Great-Aunt Jane remembers her father, Arthur, saying how he almost died of typhoid at this school. His mother was told to come to the school as fast as possible as her son might not last the day. Luckily he did survive although his mother spent several weeks at the school, nursing him back to health. The school day was long, from 9 in the morning until 4.30 in the afternoon, and then two more hours of supervised homework. In the winter the boys played football and in the summer they played cricket, a sport that Arthur Baker loved for the rest of his life.

LEAVING SCHOOL

When Lionel Baker left school, he went to London to train for a job in banking while Arthur returned to work on the family farm. As young adults, they probably read the newspapers and realised that tensions were building between the countries of Europe.

EARLS COLNE

▶ Maurice sent this postcard of Earls Colne Station to his little brother Harold in 1909. The three older brothers travelled to school by train from Lavenham.

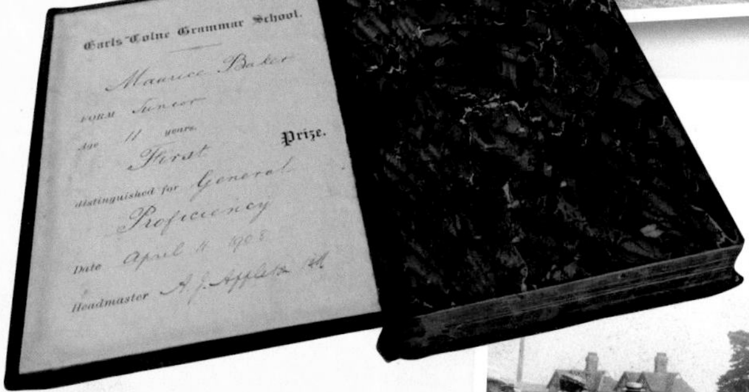
Earls Colne Grammar School.
Maurice Baker
Prize.
distinguished for
Date
Headmaster

▶ Eliza's Great-Uncle Lionel found a book on his shelves that Maurice won as a school prize.

▶ A faded photo shows Lionel Baker winning a race at the school sports' day in 1906. He sent the photo as a postcard to his father with the words, 'Dear Father, I hope you will like this. The boy just coming in is me.'

WAR BREAKS OUT, 1914

Eliza found a reference to the outbreak of the First World War in the farm diary kept by her great-great grandfather. Most of the diary is concerned with the farm but a few other events are recorded.

1914
June, July and August very hot and dry –
quite a drought.
Excellent Harvest weather and generally a
good crop of corn excepting spring beans.
Sept 12/14 the first nice rain for several hours,
followed by a fine dry Sunday.
War declared at commencement of Harvest.

THE COMING OF WAR

During the long, hot summer of 1914, tensions between countries in Europe reached a crisis. Almost all the countries of Europe were linked together by alliances (agreements) to give each other support in the event of invasion or attack by another country. When Archduke Franz Ferdinand, heir to the Austrian throne, was assassinated on 28th June, this led to Austria-Hungary declaring war on Serbia a month later. By 4th August, when Britain declared war on Germany, Germany was already at war with Russia and France, and had invaded Belgium. Although legally Britain did not have to go to war, it had promised to defend Belgium under the Treaty of London, 1839.

BRITISH EXPEDITIONARY FORCE

Britain's small professional army crossed the English Channel to support the French army in fighting the Germans in Belgium. Called the British Expeditionary Force (BEF), it consisted of around 120,000 men, soon to be joined by members of the Territorial Force (TF), who had been part-time soldiers. Several battles took place yet neither side could push for victory. By November, each side had dug defensive trenches stretching from the North Sea to Switzerland.

▼ The Cavalry Division of the BEF retreats from the Battle of Mons, August 1914. This was the first battle fought between the German and British armies.

MAIN PICTURE: Volunteers queue to join the armed forces in August, 1914. Over 400,000 had joined by 10 September.

JOINING UP AND CONSCRIPTION

In a wave of patriotism, thousands of men rushed to enlist at recruiting offices all over the country, including Lionel Baker, who left his job in banking to join the University and Public Schools Brigade in 1914. His brother Maurice enlisted in April 1915. Much later he told his niece that the Kitchener poster (see centre right) had influenced his decision. In 1916, yet more recruits were needed so conscription was introduced for unmarried men aged between 18 and 41, and soon included married men as well. Men received official 'call-up' letters asking them to register with the armed forces.

▶ Lionel Baker, 21 by now, joined the University and Public Schools Brigade to train as an army officer.

▼ Lord Kitchener, Secretary of State for War, stares out from this famous recruitment poster. Kitchener made a big impression on young men, who volunteered in their thousands for the armed services.

▼ Members of the Territorial Force gather in Lavenham market place on 5th August 1914 to set off for war, which had only been declared hours before. The same scene was repeated all across the country.

ARTHUR'S WAR

Eliza's great-grandfather, Arthur Baker, was 19 when war broke out in 1914. Eliza's granny recalls that her father, Arthur, desperately wanted to join up but his father forbade it, saying that he needed his help on the farm. When conscription came in 1916, Arthur was not called up as his job in farming was exempt – his war effort was needed at home.

▲ Pages from the farm diary kept by Arthur's father.

ON THE FARM

It was vital that farmers continued to grow crops and raise livestock during the war to feed the British people and to provide rations for soldiers. Before the war, Britain had imported large quantities of food supplies from abroad but now Britain needed to produce most of its food itself. Eliza looked at the farm diary kept by her great-great grandfather, John Baker, to find out what he and Arthur grew on their farm. The diary mentions barley, wheat, oats, beans, peas, mangold and swede. They fed mangold and swede, both root vegetables, to their cattle and pigs, as well as to the working horses. The Bakers owned several horses to pull farm equipment.

▶ This poster asks British people to save food, thus helping the war effort. The Royal Navy tried to protect the ships which brought food to Britain but many were sunk by German submarines.

◀ Bringing in the mangold harvest. Farm workers pulled up the mangold plants by hand and piled them up, ready to load onto a cart.

DO YOUR BIT
SAVE·FOOD

RISING FOOD PRICES

The farm diary tracks the rising cost of food in the price of wheat. The Baker family were selling wheat at 20 shillings per coomb, an old measurement of corn by volume, in 1914, and for 39 shillings per coomb two years later. The high prices pushed up the cost of bread so much that some people were struggling to feed their families. Eventually, in 1918, certain foods were rationed to share out food supplies across all the people of Britain. It is unlikely that the Bakers, as farmers and millers, suffered from food shortages themselves.

▲ Loading the hay on to a horse-drawn cart. Hay was much in demand during the war since huge amounts were needed in France to feed all the horses used by the army.

THE ARTISTS RIFLES

Arthur volunteered for the Artists Rifles, part of the Territorial Force, along with friends from Lavenham Cricket Club. This meant that he was a part-time soldier and full-time farmer. Members of the Territorial Force were issued with a uniform and a gun, and they attended summer training camps. Although many from the Territorial Force did become full-time soldiers and went on to fight abroad, the role of others, including Arthur, was to defend the local area, should there be a German invasion.

◄ Arthur's winning score is fifth from the top.

▼ Arthur (far right) has the highest score on the board at this army shooting competition in 1918.

MAURICE'S WAR

Maurice Baker

ELIZA'S GREAT-GREAT UNCLE MAURICE WAS ONLY 17 IN 1914. He was training to be an accountant in London. The following year he joined the London Rifle Brigade as a rifleman and kept in touch with his parents by writing letters. Many of these letters have been kept safe, first by Maurice's mother, then by Maurice himself until he handed them to his niece, Eliza's Great-Aunt Jane, at the end of his long life.

1 An official photo of Maurice Baker in his uniform. Soldiers kept personal items and their paybook, a record of their wages, in the pockets. **2** Some of the envelopes that contained Maurice's letters home to his family. **3** The army identity tags that Maurice wore around his neck.

BASIC TRAINING

After Maurice enlisted in April 1915, he spent the summer at a training camp in Epsom, Surrey. There he learnt how to use a rifle and a bayonet, march, follow orders, dig trenches, and perform basic first aid. Recruits spent a lot of time doing fitness training. Maurice must have sent several letters home at this time but hardly any have survived. Eliza did read this one with a postmark of 12th August, 1915, where Maurice tells his mother that he will be coming home next weekend:

Learning to use a bayonet

R'fn G. M. Baker. 2045
B Company, London Rifle Brigade
Tadworth Camp, Epsom

Dear Mother
You will be pleased (no doubt) to hear that I shall be coming home this week end & return Monday afternoon. I managed to get extension of leave. I was very surprised we were inspected today by Major General Boyle. I am practically spent out & shall not draw enough on Friday to get me home. I should be very pleased with a little assistance but do not send a cheque, I should not be able to change it.
In haste
Your affect. Son, Maurice

Drill training at Tadworth Camp

LEAVING FOR FRANCE

Another surviving letter warns his parents that he will be leaving for active service in France shortly – he has been 'warned for the next draft'. He is worried about whether his age (18) will prevent him from being sent into action – 'I had expected to be left out on account of age'. Recruits had to be at least 18 but they were not supposed to be sent abroad until they had reached the age of 19. Often the army overlooked this fact, as they did in the case of Maurice. Maurice also appears to have lost some uniform, his tunic and breeches.

Postmark: Epsom 29th September 1915
3rd Battn. London Rifle Brigade
Tadworth, Surrey
Wednesday

Dear Mother & Father

I have (you may be pleased to hear) been warned for the next draft. I have been before the Medical Officer. They know my exact age but as I have absolutely nothing wrong with me I shall go. Of course they might make an 11th hour decision & chuck me out, or the draft might not go. You don't know how pleased I was when I heard my name read out. I had expected to be left out on account of age, & to be left behind & all the pals I know go out would be absolutely rotten.

You may expect me home for 4 days leave by any train. I expect I shall come home tomorrow. We were inspected by Major-General Boyle this morning.

It's not my fault about the tunic & breeches. I had a card from Nash to say he had sent them off on the Wednesday. They were not there at 5 p.m. on the Saturday. I went to Rainham Station. Have written to Rainham Station Master.

Your loving Son
Maurice

P.S Very likely see you tomorrow have given all details about 4 days leave

◀ Many men failed medicals due to poor eyesight, a weak chest or general ill-health. Here, a chair is used to check a man's weight, while another man's height is measured.

In one of his last letters written in England, Maurice captures the moment when he is about to set off for active service in France:

Postmark Southampton 13th October 1915
Rfn. G. M. Baker 2045
Wednesday   5th London Rifle Brigade,
Rest Camp, Southampton

Dear Mother

We arrived here yesterday & are waiting for the boat to take us across the water. This is a very nice camp, thirty in a hut which would hold fifty quite comfortably. We fetched rifles & bayonets this morning. No one knows when we shall be off, all drafts generally stay here 2-3 or 4 days. It's very nice here not much to do – hope to go to the hippodrome tonight.

Your affect. Son

Maurice

Soldiers queue to board a troop ship.

DEAR MOTHER

MAURICE CONTINUED TO WRITE LETTERS TO HIS PARENTS from France, especially his mother. Many of the letters respond to his mother's worries about how he is managing and ask for various items to be sent to France.

◄ A soldier reads letters from home.

FOOD, CIGARETTES, MONEY

Maurice often asks for food and money and always asks for cigarettes.

▲ Canadian soldiers take a daytime nap, while their companion writes a letter. Cigarettes helped to pass the time as well.

30th Oct
Dear Mother,
I'm very well. My appetite seems to have increased since I am over. A lot of the fellows have a parcel sent out every week. You might send out a small one every week. I can not get cigarettes at all where we are now. We're miles from anywhere. You might send a tin of 50 every week. For some reason or other we're not supposed to put our address at the top. My correct address is

> *Rifleman G. M. Baker*
> *11 Platoon, C. Company*
> *L.R.B.   BEF*

Chocolate is jolly good stuff too. Cadbury's Mexican choc is about best. You could also send out that stove affair & a few walnuts. I got the Scarf. It is just A.1. We're getting quite good grub here.
> *There is no news whatever.*
> *Your affect. Son*
> *Maurice*

▼ As the front line had to be guarded at all times, soldiers ate their meals in the trenches in all weathers.

▲ Soldiers of the London Rifle Brigade, which Maurice belonged to, are well wrapped up against the cold in early 1915. As well as the cold, soldiers had to cope with mud and rain in the trenches where they spent weeks of their lives.

These requests were written in different letters:

You might also send out a pheasant, or some partridges or even a chicken already cooked & the etc's. I hear a very good way to keep them fresh is to put slices of raw onion all over the chicken or pheasant.

In parcels, if you always send cigarettes, chocolate, cake, potted meat. I don't know whether you can get them or not, but breakfast sausages are jolly good. A lot of the fellows have them sent out.

Thanks very much for the £1. I got 28 francs for it at a Canteen out here. There is no need for you to send out 7/- a week. 2/6 a week is quite enough to help with the pay I draw. (2/6 means 2 shillings and 6 pence.)

Maurice also asks for lice powder to kill these irritating insects that lived in soldiers' clothes, bit them and made their skin sore and itchy.

Thanks very much for Lice powder. I am free of them now but send out some more. It's very easy to get rid of lice for a day or 2 but permanently is a different thing. They lay so many eggs.

▲ Maurice mentions estaminets, small French cafés, in his letter reproduced on the right. Soldiers relaxed at these cafes when they were away from the trenches.

MAURICE'S DAY

In this letter, Maurice describes his life while answering some of his mother's questions. He compares life in the trenches with where he is staying at the time, in a barn in the French countryside.

Dec. 6th 1915
Dear Mother,
I will start by answering your few questions.
(1) We get up fairly late & before going into trenches we used to do a march during the day or work to keep us fit.
(2) We have food just the same as we had in England. Bacon for breakfast. Generally stew for dinner, & we have had cheese & jam. Tea's served at breakfast & tea. The food is cooked better as a rule than we had in England.
(3) We wash every day. In the trenches of course you cannot always.
(4) I take most of my clothes off at night. We've got 2 blankets each now. Until last night we had only had one each.
(5) Already answered.
(6) There are Estaminets every week where you can get coffee & French beer & in some of them omelettes & chips. These estaminets are very numerous, every third house is either a shop or an estaminet. We are allowed in these estaminets from 11 till 1 & from 6 pm till 8 pm.
(7) We have to be back in our billets by 8.30 pm & generally in bed by 9.
(8) We sleep on the floor & very comfy too when one is tired.
(9) I do not want an air pillow. I sleep quite happily with my pack as a pillow.
(The letter continues.)

On 12th February 1916 Maurice signed off a letter:

So long, Goodnight, Your loving Son
Maurice
P.S. I hope I'm not too much of a worry to you. Really if you look at it in the right light, I'm not much to worry about.

ON ACTIVE SERVICE.

▲ Envelopes printed with the words ON ACTIVE SERVICE were handed out once or twice a week for soldiers to send letters home. A censor checked letters for information that might be useful to the Germans.

ON ACTIVE SERVICE

SOLDIERS WERE NOT ALLOWED TO WRITE MILITARY SECRETS in their letters, in case the letters fell into German hands, but they could describe their lives. Eliza and her mother can follow Maurice's movements back and forth from the front line in his letters. This extract comes from one written on 6th December 1915:

The usual procedure is 6 days in various trenches, 6 days back resting, getting clean, removing mud. Out of the 6 days in trenches, 4 days are in reserve & 2 days in firing line trench. So our turn in trenches occurs every 12 days. We are at a fairly quiet part of the line.

THE WESTERN FRONT

For millions of soldiers, including Maurice and his brother Lionel, their experience of war was in the trenches on the Western Front in Belgium and France. The Western Front was a system of trenches dug by the French and British armies on one side and the German army on the other, to protect their soldiers. The aim of the generals on both sides was to push the front line of their trenches forwards, capture land held by the enemy and eventually win the war. In reality, there was little movement along the front line for much of the war.

IN THE TRENCHES

Once in France, Maurice and the other soldiers continued to train, took it in turns to be in the front or reserve line of trenches, dug or repaired trenches, brought up supplies and eventually earned some rest at a camp set back from the action.

▲ A typical trench was around two metres deep, with sandbags for protection from enemy fire. The sentry stood or knelt on a fire step, keeping watch.

▲ Soldiers dig a communication trench in 1915. Communication trenches linked front line and reserve line trenches to camps further back and were used to move men and supplies back and forth.

On the 23rd December, 1915, Maurice sent this letter to his parents:

Dear Mother & Father,
A pal who is going on leave is posting this letter for me in England. We are going to have a good time this Xmas. We are out of the trenches. We came out on the evening of the 21st & are out for 8 days.

[Further down the letter he wrote:]

At our point of the line the trenches we hold, there is not a lot of danger. It is surprising how casually everyone takes things up in the trenches. I had imagined myself feeling very funny round the gills when shells come over. They have shelled us 3 or 4 times with a few small shells at different times. All you do is to keep down low, light a cigarette & wait till they finish. Nobody seems to be frightened. I have felt worse in England many times on a dark night when the birds suddenly rustle in the bushes. Unless one of those shells falls right into the trench no danger is done to anybody & only about 1 shell in 50 falls into the trench. When they send Shrapnel over you get into your bivvy, i.e. a dug out which has sand bags & earth on top of it. More than sufficient to stop a piece of falling Shrapnel. Of course the worse part of it is the hardship & that is not wonderfully great. While in the front line you cannot sleep a lot but you are never in the front line for more than 3 days, or generally 2 days.

On 31st January 1916 Maurice told his mother that he was a sniper, chosen for this job because he was particularly good at shooting.

Where we snipe from is the front line with special steel plated loopholes & we are 400 yds away from the German trenches. On the 2nd Morning I and another fellow are practically certain we got a Hun. He ran along the parapet for about 3 or 4 yds. It was just light & about 400 yds away. We had three shots each, in rapid succession when he suddenly went down, & we saw no more of him. Yesterday was very misty & we could not see the German line & shooting was out of the question.

▲ A soldier checks hand grenades next to sandbags piled up at the entrance to a dug-out in a trench.

After several weeks in the trenches, soldiers were sent to rest camps back from the front line. On 19th March Maurice wrote:

Then we moved to a glorious village within a mile of a town a bit bigger than Bury St. Eds. I had 2 nice dinners in that town. We had glorious weather, as we have had for last week. A crystal clear stream ran at the back of our billets & we lay out there in the sun. I did some clothes washing there. It was a great success.

▶ Maurice had this photo taken to send home and mentions it in his letter of 18th March:

I had my photo taken on Sunday so will send you one in about 3 weeks time. I'm not having a bad time at all.

ATTACK!

In the week leading up to 1st July 1916, when his battalion was based close to the River Somme, Maurice must have been deafened by the noise of the British guns bombarding the German lines in preparation for a big attack.

▼ British guns rained shells down on the German front line in late June 1916, to put their machine guns and defences out of action and make it safer for British troops to attack.

THE BATTLE OF THE SOMME

The aim of the battle was to break the deadlock of the previous months of trench warfare. General Haig of the British Army had a plan to attack along a 32-km-stretch of the Western Front, break through the German front line and win the war. Maurice and men of the London Rifle Brigade were attacking at the north of the Somme battlefield to create a diversion and distract the Germans from the main attack to the south.

▶ Canadian soldiers shelter from shrapnel in a trench during the Battle of the Somme, 1916.

6.55am

Eliza's mother talked to her uncle about Maurice's memories of 1st July 1916. Maurice and some other soldiers were waiting for the whistle to signal the attack when a German shell exploded above them, killing five immediately

and wounding Maurice and one other soldier. Maurice once told his nephew, with tears in his eyes, that, due to being so badly wounded, he was in no position to help the other wounded man, who soon died. Maurice managed to drag himself along on his elbows to reach medical help at the Regimental Aid Post.

Maurice wrote of the attack in this letter to his mother, written on 8th July:

… Our Battn. got cut up badly I'm afraid. We made an attack to draw the enemy's forces. We drew them all right. The noise was terrible. Just before we were going over a shell burst right on top of us. Killed 5. Wounded the rest. That is how I got wounded.

▲ A wounded soldier receives medical help in a trench on 1st July 1916.

1ST JULY AND BEYOND

On the first day of the Battle of the Somme, 20,000 British soldiers were killed and nearly 40,000 were injured. It turned out that the bombardment of the German front line before the attack had not managed to destroy German defences as General Haig had planned, so when the British soldiers started to walk across No Man's Land they were mown down by German gunfire. Despite heavy losses, the fighting continued until bad weather brought it to a halt in mid-November. By then, the British and French armies had gained little ground and the war was far from over. Over a million men from both sides were injured or killed in these battles.

▼ Soldiers make their way through the barbed wire in No Man's Land in August 1916, in the continuing Battle of the Somme.

BAD NEWS

MAURICE REACHED THE REGIMENTAL AID POST HIMSELF, where stretcher-bearers carried him back to a Dressing Station. During this short journey he was wounded again, in the shoulder. He would have been taken to a Casualty Clearing Station at this point and on to the base hospital.

▲ A doctor treats wounded men at a Regimental Aid Post in 1917. All the armies involved in the war had army medical corps. They ran Regimental Aid Posts, Dressing Stations, Casualty Clearing Stations and base hospitals.

IN HOSPITAL

Maurice's letters from hospital tell the story of what happened next. Maurice was more badly wounded than it had seemed at first.

July 4th 1916

Dear Mother,

I am down in a base hospital with wounds (Shrapnel) in leg & foot. I shan't be able to walk for some time. I am being treated very well & in spite of everything not doing so bad. We had a hot time up the line. I was hit very early on in the operations. Just as we were about to go over the top. I'm in a most awkward position for writing so I'll chuck it up. You need not worry at all about me. I'm going on alright.

Maurice

◀ Maurice's original letter is shown here, with the transcript. He talks about being wounded 'as we were about to go over the top' which is how soldiers talked about leaving the safety of the trench or shell crater, in Maurice's case, to form part of the attack on the German front line.

MEDICAL TREATMENT

After a month at the Canadian army hospital in France, Maurice travelled on a hospital ship to England, and by train to a hospital in Glasgow to recover from his wounds. His leg was slow to heal but he was eventually transported to Brettenham Park in Suffolk to continue his recovery closer to home. Maurice remained at Brettenham Park, waiting for his amputated leg to heal but it was infected.

Dear Mother,

July 6th

I have a little bad news for you. I have lost my right leg. It is amputated below the knee. I expect I shall find it a bit awkward with a cork leg at first. I hope the villagers of Lavenham will not want to do the same to me as they did to the fellow Parker who lost a leg. Send the band down and be shouted at by Religious men of all denominations.

As soon as my leg is well enough for me to move I hope to return to England.

My address is

Rfn G. M. Baker
No 3 Ward
VII Canadian General Hospital
France

Ah Well , Your loving Son
Maurice

◀ Maurice drew this picture of himself on a letter to his cousins in London.

▲ In this letter Maurice gives his mother the bad news about his leg. Not wanting any fuss, he hopes that the 'band', the Salvation Army marching band, will not use his return as a focus for their attention.

▶ A photo of soldiers recovering at Brettenham Park, a Red Cross hospital for wounded soldiers based in a huge private house. Maurice was moved here at the end of October 1916.

▼ On 3rd August, 1917, Maurice was officially discharged from the army due to being 'no longer physically fit for war service'.

Over a year later, in December 1917, doctors at the Military Hospital in London had to operate on Maurice again. This time his leg was amputated to mid-thigh. By then he had learnt to walk with crutches and was eventually fitted with a wooden leg. He returned home to live with his parents and his brothers, Arthur and Harold, until he was strong enough to go out to work.

Army Form E. 511.

If this certificate is lost or mislaid no duplicate of it can be obtained.

DISCHARGE CERTIFICATE OF A SOLDIER OF THE TERRITORIAL FORCE.

This is to certify that (No.) 301277 (Rank) Rifleman

(Name) George Maurice BAKER

(Unit) LONDON RIFLE BRIGADE who was enlisted to serve in the Territorial Force of the County of London

on the Twenty first day of April 1915, is discharged in consequence of *Being no longer physically fit for war service, under para 392 xvi King's Regulations and that his claims have been properly settled.

His total service in the Territorial Force is 2 years 105 days, including 2 years 105 days embodied service.

Service abroad, viz., in France years 240 days.

Medals, Clasps, and Decorations

LIONEL'S WAR

Lionel Baker

BACK AT THE HOUSE OF HER GREAT-UNCLE LIONEL IN LAVENHAM, Eliza looked at all sorts of war-related papers belonging to her Great-Great Uncle Lionel, Maurice's eldest brother. He joined the army in 1914 and remained in the army after the end of the war, often serving abroad. He stored some of his belongings with relatives in Suffolk.

◀ An army portrait of Lionel, 1914.

TRAINING TO BE AN OFFICER

Lionel joined the University and Public Schools Brigade to train to be an officer. Officer training was longer than the training for an ordinary soldier so his brother Maurice reached active service in France ahead of him, even though he joined up nine months later.

THE SUFFOLKS

Training complete, Lionel joined the 2nd Battalion of the Suffolk Regiment as a 2nd Lieutenant in charge of between 25 and 40 men, a platoon. He was sent to France in February 1916 and, like his brother Maurice, he fought on the Western Front. He was wounded the next month and returned home to recover, a 'blighty' wound, as Maurice described it, in one of his letters home in March 1916:

How is Lionel getting on? By the way you wrote it didn't seem a bad wound, just a "Blighty" touch. Blighty is England. No one talks of England out here, it is always Blighty.

▲ Lionel Baker (seated right) and officers of the Suffolk Regiment in 1916. A dog, possibly the regimental mascot, must have moved, creating the strange shape in the foreground.

BACK TO FRANCE

The farm diary kept by the brothers' father shows that their parents had an eventful August in 1916. By this time Maurice was in hospital in Glasgow while his brother Lionel, now recovered from his lesser wound, prepared to return to France. The diary suggests that the brothers' father left Glasgow early in order to see his eldest son, Lionel, in London's Hyde Park before his departure for France once more.

Went to see Maurice at Glasgow from 16th to 29th August.
Returned to London on 26th August Bush H[yde] Park.
Lionel left for France on August 28th.

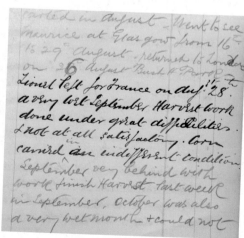

▲ The farm diary page for August, 1916.

PROMOTION

Lionel was now an acting Captain, in charge of three or four platoons (up to 200 men). Soon he was in action close to where Maurice had been wounded earlier in the year. There is one surviving letter from Lionel, see right.

Although he was an officer, Lionel slept in a cellar with his men. The letter doesn't say what the working parties were doing. They could have been trying to find out what the Germans were up to, or they may have been repairing or digging trenches, rolling out defensive wire or taking up supplies.

B.E.F.
France
20th Oct 1916

Dear Father & Mother,
I have not written lately because I have been too busy for words. We were about four miles behind the firing line but practically lived in the trenches because we had to take working parties up about every day and sometimes twice, then we went to another place for two days and are now about two miles behind firing line. We sleep in a cellar & just behind this house there is a battery of fairly large guns which nearly shake the house down every time they fire. Thank you very much for the socks. The tanks are quite a success. I saw about a hundred the other day in their "Park".
(The letter continues.)

There is no more news
Your loving son,
Lionel.

▲ Lionel's letter mentions the battery of guns close to the cellar where he sleeps. Here a shell is being loaded into a howitzer. When these shells exploded they caused death and destruction.

▲ Lionel's letter doesn't say what his working party did. This photo shows a working party trying to dig a tank out of a captured German trench.

◄ Lionel kept this photo showing officers enjoying a picnic in the French countryside. He is the man sitting side on in the centre of the photo.

LIONEL'S BOX

In a cardboard box marked *LIONEL*, Eliza and her mother found an envelope containing photos from the Imperial War Museum and some other official photographs. We don't know whether Lionel went to the Imperial War Museum at some point after the war to research the photos or how he came to get them, but perhaps they are the war as he remembered it. He kept these photos all his life and some of them are reproduced here.

◀ A snapshot of Lionel Baker seated outside his tent.

▲ Ruined buildings in the town of Arras, France, 1917.

▼ A padre holds a service for the burial of soldiers, 1917.

▲ Casualty Clearing Station surrounded by men on stretchers.

▼ Soldiers preparing to move forward from reserve trenches during the Battle of Arras, 1917.

THE BATTLE OF ARRAS

Most of the photos relate to the Battle of Arras in April/May 1917. A quick search on the Internet brought up a strong link between the Battle of Arras and the Suffolk Regiment, in which Lionel served. The Battle of Arras had the heaviest daily casualty figure of any battle in the whole war.

LIONEL'S POCKETS

Early on in the Battle of Arras, in April 1917, Lionel was wounded again. Perhaps because of this injury, four tatty military message notes dated 10th and 11th April have survived. Maybe they were folded up in one of his uniform pockets when he was taken back to a field hospital to recover. These messages carry the orders of the commanding officer, delivered on foot by a runner to junior officers. One says: *Latest information not move tomorrow evening. The 3rd army has up to now taken 160 guns and 6,000 prisoners. No news of the French.* Another says: *All men will change their socks before we move tomorrow if possible and duty socks to be collected and sent to HQ.* Officers had to look after the soldiers' feet as trench foot, caused by wearing damp socks and leaky boots, led to soldiers needing urgent medical attention.

MILITARY CROSS

Lionel was awarded the Military Cross (left) after the Battle of Arras. A brief description of his actions was published in the *London Gazette*, July 1917: *For conspicuous gallantry and devotion to duty. He led his company with the greatest skill and courage. He organised a bombing attack on the enemy trench which was still holding out. His disregard for danger was an example to all, and contributed largely to the final success.*

▲ One of the military message notes kept by Lionel, and his field message book (right).

▼ A photo of Lionel Baker (right) and other officers taken around the time of the Battle of Arras.

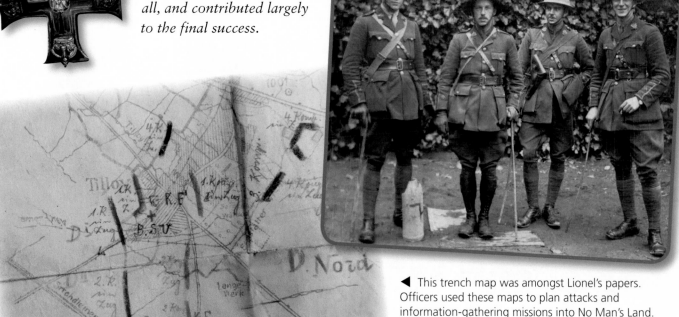

◀ This trench map was amongst Lionel's papers. Officers used these maps to plan attacks and information-gathering missions into No Man's Land.

1918

WITH THE WAR NOW IN ITS FOURTH YEAR, CAPTAIN LIONEL BAKER was still commanding men on the Western Front in France. Eliza had to rely on her mother to tell her what happened next.

▲ Thousands of German troops attacked the British front line in March 1918. Here German troops advance through the devastated streets of St Quentin, following the order to attack.

THE SPRING OFFENSIVES

The German army took the upper hand early in 1918 and launched a series of successful attacks on the British and French armies along the Western Front. Still based around the French town of Arras, Lionel's battalion tried to repel this advance in March 1918. The scene is described in *The History of the Suffolk Regiment*, and tells how Captain Simpson and Captain Baker and their men became surrounded by the Germans but they kept on fighting until they had run out of ammunition, when they were forced to surrender.

Their struggle was reported in *The Times*:

"There is a story, such as painters ought to make immortal and historians to celebrate, of how certain Suffolks, cut off and surrounded, fought back to back on the Wancourt-Tilloy road."

The 'certain Suffolks' mentioned in the newspaper were led by Captain Lionel Baker and his fellow officer. Back home in Lavenham, Lionel's parents received a letter from his commanding officer telling them that their son was missing.

PRISONER OF WAR

Captain Lionel Baker was missing but he was not dead. Soon his family received news that he had been taken prisoner and was in a prisoner of war (POW) camp in Germany. He kept a diary at this time in a German notebook. At first he wrote every day but then not quite so regularly.

He began the diary on 28th March:

Bombardment of back areas started at 3 am, intense. At 3.15 bombardment of trench system commenced exceptionally intense which lasted until about 7 am. Was taken prisoner about 8.30 am after having had a lot of firing at the enemy, who eventually got in the trench on our left flank owing to the retirement of the Division.

The diary entries follow Lionel's slow progress through German-occupied France into Germany, by foot and by train. A week later they arrived at a POW camp in Rastatt, Germany. To Lionel's disappointment, conditions were very basic in the camp and they lived off small amounts of bread and vegetable soup.

*April 6
Bread issue here 5 to a loaf. Breakfast coffee, lunch soup at 11.30 am, tea at 4.30 pm & soup at 6 pm.*

On 11th April Lionel wrote: *Felt very weak owing perhaps to the hot weather.* A month later, on 19th May, he has been moved to a proper camp at Mainz:

Mainz is much better than Rastatt which now seems like a nightmare.

But Lionel is still not receiving enough food to eat and documents:

Going up & down stairs to meals is more than enough exercise. [21st May]
The stairs here are a huge effort. Have never been as thin before in my life or felt so weak. [31st May]

Most of the diary entries up until then record how little he has eaten but on 24th July he records:

Felt very fit & cheerful, especially as I received 3 letters this morning.

Lionel stopped writing his diary on 24th August, 1918.

VICTORY

Lionel was captured when the Germans tried to take the advantage and finish the war in their favour. This failed and the British and French armies, now helped by the Americans, who had joined the war in 1917, had much success in later 1918, eventually winning the war. The fighting stopped at 11 o'clock on 11th November, 1918. Back in the POW camp, Lionel and the other prisoners were free to make their way across Europe and return home.

◀ Far left: Lionel was in a POW camp for officers in Mainz and recorded that his photo had been taken on 1st July. Lionel is standing on the right.

◀ The prisoners staged plays in the Mainz camp to keep themselves busy.

THE CAMP DRAMATIC SOCIETY
PRESENTS
THREE EPISODES FROM
"THE HEART OF PRINCESS OSRA"
PRECEDED BY
A ONE ACT FARCE
THE CASTAWAY
PRICE ·20

Programme
MAINZ
P.O.W.
CAMP THEATRE

REMEMBRANCE

MORE THAN NINE MILLION SERVICE PEOPLE HAD DIED across the world during the war, including 76 young men from Lavenham. Inside Lavenham Church there is a memorial to these soldiers with all their names carved in stone. Lionel and Maurice Baker's names could easily have been there.

◄ The war memorial in Lavenham Church was unveiled in 1920. The book of remembrance, finished in 1922, sits on the wooden table beneath the memorial.

BOOK OF REMEMBRANCE

In 1922 the vicar of Lavenham organised a book called *The Dead who died for England*, so 'that something more than their mere names, may be known of the Lavenham men who gave their lives for their country in the Great War'. People can turn the pages to read about each dead soldier in turn. On George Pryke's page it is written, 'He was one of seven brothers who joined the Army.' Three of the Pryke brothers never came home – Thomas (died 1916), George (died 1917) and Charles (died 1918). On the same street as the Baker family, the Kemp family lost James Jubilee Kemp, who died in the Battle of the Somme on the same day as Maurice was wounded – 1 July, 1916.

► Eliza looks at the entry for James Kemp in Lavenham Church's book of remembrance. Kemp was killed on the same day as her Great-Great Uncle was injured.

Kemp. James Jubilee.   31 Prentice Street

*Enlisted, May 1915, in Royal Garrison Artillery.
Trained at Dover.
Went to France, June 1916.
Killed on Somme, July 1st 1916.
As signaller he obtained highest marks.
He was killed with two others while resting asleep in a shell hole.
The New Testament in his pocket was pierced by a piece of shrapnel.*

MEMORIALS

Along with those inside churches, war memorials were erected in churchyards, high streets, school halls, villages and public buildings. On 11th November, 1920, the Cenotaph memorial was unveiled in London's Whitehall. Since then it has been the focus of the Remembrance Day Service held each November. Also that year, an unidentified body of a soldier killed in France was reburied in Westminster Abbey to represent all of the unidentified soldiers killed during the First World War.

FIRST WORLD WAR CEMETERIES

Hardly any of the men listed on the memorial and in *The Dead who died for England* in Lavenham Church are buried in the cemetery, except for a few who died of their injuries back in England. Soldiers were usually buried close to where they died, mostly in cemeteries in France. Using the website of the Commonwealth War Graves Commission, Eliza and her mother looked up James Jubilee Kemp to find out where he is buried.

▲ Originally built in wood, the Cenotaph was remade in stone and unveiled on 11th November, 1920.

Plot 1. Row G.	BERTRANCOURT
Grave 12	MILITARY CEMETERY

▼ Rows of gravestones stand in a First World War cemetery at Vimy Ridge, near Arras, France. Each is marked with the name and rank of the dead soldier. Unknown soldiers have a gravestone inscribed with: A British soldier of the Great War. Known unto God.

WHAT HAPPENED NEXT?

LIONEL stayed in the army, in India and elsewhere and fought in the Second World War. By this time he was a Lieutenant Colonel in Malaya, where he was taken prisoner once again. Despite great hardships, he survived and returned home. He died in 1976.

ARTHUR remained a farmer and miller all his life in Lavenham, in partnership with his youngest brother, Harold. Arthur was in the Home Guard during the Second World War. He married Jessie, Eliza's great-granny in 1937, had four children, 13 grandchildren, and was buried in Lavenham Cemetery in 1981.

MAURICE recovered at home with his parents, returned to London to learn to be an accountant, worked at an agricultural college, tried farming and eventually worked in a local business. He married in his 60s and reached the age of 100, dying in 1997.

HAROLD, the youngest of the Baker brothers, was still at school when the war ended. He went into partnership with his brother Arthur, and served in the Royal Observor Corps during the Second World War. He married Betty, had two sons and four grandsons. He lived in Suffolk all his life and died in 1983.

▲ Lionel dressed in uniform during the 1920s or 1930s.

▶ Arthur, Jessie and their children on a day out to the seaside in the early 1950s. Eliza's granny, also named Jessie, is the girl standing in front of her mother.

▶ Far right: Maurice in later life – at the seaside with his brother Harold's son, John.

SOME USEFUL WEBSITES FOR RESEARCHING YOUR OWN FAMILY'S INVOLVEMENT IN THE FIRST WORLD WAR

www.iwm.org.uk/server/show/nav.6
Imperial War Museums have several downloadable guides to help you research your family history.

www.cwgc.org/
The Commonwealth War Graves Commission has a database listing the 1.7 million men and women of the Commonwealth forces who died in the two world wars and the memorials or cemeteries where they are commemorated.

http://twgpp.org/
The War Graves Photographic Project is photographing every war grave and memorial from the First World War to the present day.

www.nationalarchives.gov.uk/records/research-guides/british-army-soldiers-1914-1918.htm
Follow this link for a guide to all the documents held at The National Archives which can be used to trace First World War soldiers. However, many

GLOSSARY

A.1 Slang for 'First class, excellent'.

Active service As a soldier this means you are in the war zone rather than in a training camp back home.

Alliance A formal agreement or promise between governments.

Amputation Removing all or part of an arm or leg by surgery.

Armed forces The Army, Royal Navy, Royal Air Force.

Artillery Large guns that fire explosive shells over long distances.

Battalion An army unit made up of about 800–1,000 soldiers.

Battery A unit of artillery guns.

Battle of Arras The battle that took place around the French town of Arras between 9th April and 16th May, 1917.

Battle of the Somme The battle that took place close to the River Somme in France between 1st July and 18th November, 1916.

Bayonet A long blade fixed to the end of a rifle, used in hand-to-hand fighting.

Billets The army word for soldiers' accommodation – somewhere to sleep.

Breeches Trousers that end below the knee.

Brigade Army unit usually made up of four battalions (see above) and consisting of around 4,000 men.

Canteen The place where soldiers' meals were served.

Casualty figure The number of soldiers injured or killed.

Cavalry In the First World War, soldiers on horseback.

Censor An officer who had the job of reading soldiers' letters to make sure they did not contain any military secrets.

Conscription Being forced to join the armed forces.

Crater A huge hole in the ground caused by an explosion.

Draft Maurice uses this word to describe the group of men who have been selected to be sent to France.

Enlist Join the armed forces.

Exempt In the First World War, men who were not made to join the armed services because their work was needed at home (as farmers or miners etc) or because of their ill-health or disability.

Francs French currency used before the euro.

Gallantry Bravery.

General A senior commanding officer, in charge of an Army.

Grammar school A type of secondary school which provides an academic education.

HQ Short for headquarters.

Hippodrome A theatre showing popular shows.

Hun Nickname for a German soldier.

Identity tag Metal or cardboard disc with the soldier's army number on it.

Join up To become a member of the armed forces.

Lord Kitchener (1850-1916) The Secretary of State for War in the first years of the war. He organised the recruitment and training of huge numbers of soldiers to form new armies.

L.R.B. (London Rifle Brigade) An infantry regiment in the British Army, with its headquarters in the city of London.

No Man's Land The area of land between the two opposing front lines.

Parapet The top of the trench, on the side facing the enemy.

Patriotism Strong love of one's country.

Professional Trained and paid for the job.

Red Cross An international organisation that works to relieve suffering, whether due to a natural disaster or a war.

Regiment Basic administration unit in the British Army, divided into several Battalions.

Rifleman A soldier in a rifle regiment.

Runner A soldier who carried messages.

Second Lieutenant The lowest rank of officer in charge of 25–40 men.

Shell A metal case filled with explosives and sometimes with pieces of metal, and fired from artillery.

Shrapnel Small pieces of metal packed inside a shell (see above).

Sniper A soldier who specialises in very accurate shooting with a rifle.

Territorial Force Part of the Army made up of part-time, volunteer soldiers.

Tunic Thick jacket with pockets, worn as part of the army uniform.

Typhoid A life-threatening infectious disease.

Western Front The zone of fighting in Belgium and France that ran from the Belgian coast to the Swiss border.

First World War service records were destroyed in a bombing raid in 1940. Follow the next link created by the National Archives to find out where you can access the 1911 census for free: **www.1911census. org.uk/1911access.htm**

www.findmypast.co.uk
This is a pay-to-view website. It can be used to look at census records. A census is a record of all the people in the UK on a particular day. It usually takes place every ten years and can be used to look up people and addresses.

www.ancestry.co.uk
This is a pay-to-view website. It has several records relating to the First World War, including pension records, medal awards, service records and casualty lists. It also has census records, as well as the register of births, marriages and deaths.

www.military-genealogy.com/index.php
This is a pay-to-view website with several First World War records, including The National Roll of the Great War 1914-1918, Soldiers who died in the Great War 1914-1919 and Naval casualties 1914-1919.

INDEX